# Contents

**Editor**
Greg Payne

**Design Editor**
Liz Wright

**Origination**
Sally Robinson

**Published by**
Greenlight Publishing
The Publishing House
119 Newland Street,
Witham, Essex CM8 1WF
Tel: 01376 521900
Fax: 01376 521901
email: info@greenlightpublishing.co.uk
www.greenlightpublishing.co.uk/books

**Printed by**
Buxton Press, Derbyshire
**Button photos by**
Phase 2, Somerset

ISBN 1 897788 04 8

# Foreword

This book is not intended simply to be of interest just to collectors, nor does it simply identify a selection of civilian uniform buttons to be consulted for reference from time to time. Rather, it sets out to clarify this extensive subject by means of an original and analytical approach, and to highlight the characteristics of button design.

Hopefully, it will increase the awareness of all who read it as to the "content" of civilian uniform buttons, and convincingly demonstrate that emblem-embellished civilian uniform buttons are not just little round artefacts intended to secure clothing, but also a source of in-depth study to be appreciated and enjoyed.

Dennis G. Blair
August 2001

# Introduction

In Victorian times the adoption of distinctive uniforms came to be extended beyond military and Crown Service applications. Many civilian organisations recognised that uniforms not only served to identify "allegiances", but could also serve to emphasise authority and even generate esteem. Accordingly, it became the perpetuated norm for almost all types of uniforms to be equipped with special insignia buttons.

The examples that are shown and described in the following chapters are all British with a date range from Victorian times to the present day. The pieces included have been chosen with the purpose of providing a general review of button designs used on the attire of members of uniformed and "blazered" organisations, together with the uniforms of employees. A multitude of designs have been produced over the years. However, the selection of representative examples in this study provides a good range of design types reflecting, in many instances, "image projection", fashion, prestige and other such characteristics.

The button numbering system adopted, uses prefix initials relating to each respective chapter:-

**G** - General Overview (1-160), Chapter One

**D** - Differentiations & Updating (1-30), Chapter Two

**L** - Livery Buttons (1-72), Chapter Three

**R** - Royal Court Buttons (1-71), Chapter Four

**B** - Button Making & Backmarks (1-18), Chapter Five

**C** - Collecting Themes (1-43), Chapter Six.

# Acknowledgements

I am grateful to the many fellow button collectors who encouraged me to write this book. In particular, I thank Anne Blight, John Harris, John Richman, and Ian Scott for the information they contributed and assistance in acquiring button examples. I am also indebted to Keith C. Riddle of the BMBC, who so readily collaborated in providing technical information in respect of button making, whilst Roger Millward willingly made his research into backmarks available to me. I record my thanks too for the co-operation given by Editor Greg Payne, Publisher Alan Golbourn, and Photographer Eric Lewis.

Chapter 1

# General Overview

The examples of buttons illustrated in this section have been placed under eight category headings, A-H. Each category contains a group of 20 representative civilian uniform buttons - chosen from both past and present organisations - to help form a broad appreciation of each field. The eight categories comprise:-

**A.** National non-commercial service providers

**B.** Municipal and Utility authorities

**C.** Local Emergency and Community services

**D.** Transport operating concerns

**E.** Scholastic and Training bodies

**F.** Institutional Associations and Clubs

**G.** Sport and Leisure pursuit organisations

**H.** Commercial and Industrial businesses.

Where an organisation may be such that its field of concern spans more than one category, its classification has been determined by its perceived main function.

Although no duplicate design compositions have been included amongst these examples, it should be noted that not all bodies necessarily had individually distinctive button designs. Notably, emblem "sharing" can occur between particular services that are municipally administered, such as Fire Brigades and Ambulance Services.

Where an illustrated button design is known not to be exclusive to the accredited organisation set against it, this is indicated by the symbol "**+**" alongside its identification number. (NB Some buttons placed under the same category may fall within different theme subject groupings as demonstrated in Chapter 6). It should be noted that differences in the make-up, finishes and backmarks - of otherwise the same button as the example illustrated - often occur with the production of different issues.

## A. National Public Service Providing Organisations

These buttons have been issued by essentially non-commercial organisations, some of which were formed to support wartime efforts. They also include certain Special Police bodies.

**G.1** General Post Office

**G.2** Bank of England

**G.3** Coast Guards

**G.4** National Fire Service

**G.5** The St John's Ambulance Brigade

**G.6** Docks and Inland Waterways Executive

**G.7** British Airports Authority

**G.8** Trinity House (Lighthouse and Port Authority)

**G.9** His Majesty's Prisons

**G.10** British Broadcasting Corporation

**G.11** Royal Observer Corps

**G.12** Air Raid Precautions

**G.13** State Certified Midwives

**G.14** Women's Transport Service
(formerly First Aid Nursing Yeomanry)

**G.15** Ministry of Civil Aviation

**G.16** British Transport Docks Board

**G.17** Women's Voluntary Service

**G.18** Civil Defence

**G.19** Her Majesty's Customs

**G.20** British Museum

## G1-G20

G1

G2

G3

G4

G5

G6

G7

G8

G9

G10

G11

G12

G13

G14

G15

G16

G17

G18

G19

G20

CM

## B. Municipal & Utility Authorities

These buttons have been issued by local public services, other than transport and emergency provision.

**G.21** Metropolitan Borough of Paddington

**G.22** City of Westminster

**G.23** Corporation of West Bromwich

**G.24+** Ipswich Borough

**G.25** West Midlands Gas Board

**G.26** Nottingham Water Company

**G.27** East Midlands Electricity Board

**G.28** Southwick and Vauxhall Water Company

**G.29** Northern Lighthouses Commission

**G.30** Dartford Tunnel

**G.31** Guernsey Harbour Master

**G.32** Dover Harbour

**G.33** Port of Bristol Authority

**G.34** Port of London Authority

**G.35** Mersey Tunnel

**G.36** Manchester Ship Canal

**G.37** Thames Conservancy

**G.38** Swansea (Schools) Attendance Officer

**G.39** New River (Ware) Foreman

**G.40** Mersey Pilot Boat Service

G21-G40
CITY OF WESTMINSTER
WATER
E.M.E.B
DOVER HARBOUR
SWANSEA ATTENDANCE OFFICER
G21
G22
G23
G24
G25
G26
G27
G28
G29
G30
G31
G32
G33
G34
G35
G36
G37
G38
G39
G40
CM

## C. Local Emergency & Community Services

These buttons have been issued by organisations providing essential and care needs, principally to the public.

**G.41** Plymouth Constabulary

**G.42+** Doncaster Constabulary

**G.43** Cheshire Constabulary

**G.44** East Riding Constabulary

**G.45+** Somerset Fire Brigade

**G.46** West Midlands Fire Brigade

**G.47** Maidenhead Voluntary Fire Brigade

**G.48+** Anglesey Fire Brigade

**G.49+** Kent Ambulance Service

**G.50** London (County Council) Ambulance Service

**G.51+** Kingston-upon-Hull Ambulance Service

**G.52+** Bournemouth Ambulance Service

**G.53** Chester County Asylum

**G.54** Wolverhampton Royal Orphanage

**G.55** Edinburgh Blind Asylum

**G.56** Cane Hill Asylum

**G.57+** York City Hospital

**G.58** Bancroft's Hospital

**G.59** Sir Thomas Rich's Hospital (Gloucester)

**G.60** St Bartholomew's Hospital

G41-G60
G41
CONSTABULARY
G42
DON
G43
G44
G45
G46
WEST MIDLANDS
FIRE SERVICE
G47
G48
G49
G50
G51
G52
G53
COUNTY ASYLUM
CHESTER
G54
ROYAL ORPHANAGE
1850
G55
G56
CANE HILL
L.C.A
ASYLUM
G57
G58
1728
BANCROFTS HOSPITAL
G59
G60
CM

## D. Transport Operating Concerns - Private & Corporate

Catering for the needs of passengers and/or freight.

**G.61+** Liverpool City Corporation (buses)

**G.62** Glasgow Corporation Transport (buses)

**G.63+** Leeds City (buses)

**G.64** Westcliff on Sea (buses)

**G.65** London Transport
(buses, trolley buses, and underground)

**G.66** Swansea and Mumbles (Tramway)

**G.67** Bristol Tramcar & Carriage Co Ltd

**G.68** Portsmouth Corporation Tramways

**G.69** London Brighton & South Coast Railway

**G.70** London Midland & Scottish Railway

**G.71** Taff Vale Railway

**G.72** Midland Railway

**G.73** British India Steam Navigation Co

**G.74** Royal Mail Steam Packet Company

**G.75** Peninsular and Oriental Line

**G.76** Cunard Shipping Line

**G.77** Shell Transport & Trading Company

**G.78** Chart Air

**G.79** British European Airways

**G.80** British Overseas Airways Corporation

G61-G80
G61
GLASGOW CORPORATION TRANSPORT DEPT
G62
G63
Westcliff on Sea
G64
G65
G66
BHCL
G67
PORTSMOUTH CORPORATION TRAMWAYS
G68
LB&SC
RAILWAY
G69
LONDON MIDLAND & SCOTTISH RAILWAY COMPANY
G70
TAFF VALE RAILWAY
G71
MIDLAND
RAILWAY
G72
G73
G74
G75
G76
G77
G78
BEA
G79
G80
CM

## E. Education & Training Bodies

Private and public concerns providing teaching and instruction in the furtherance of knowledge and skills.

**G.81** University of Cambridge

**G.82** University of Liverpool

**G.83** New College Oxford

**G.84** Eton College

**G.85** Liverpool College

**G.86** Christ's Hospital School

**G.87** Highgate School

**G.88** Great Yarmouth Grammar School

**G.89** Harrow School

**G.90** Oxford University Officers' Training Corps

**G.91** Colwyn Bay Wireless College

**G.92** British Red Cross Society

**G.93** Worcester Training Ship

**G.94** Seamen's Education Service

**G.95** Boy Scouts' Association

**G.96** Girls' Venture Corps

**G.97** Sea Cadets' Corps

**G.98** Air Training Corps

**G.99** Church Lads Brigade

**G.100** Crusaders

G81-G100
G81
G82
G83
G84
GREAT YARMOUTH 1551 GRAMMAR SCHOOL
G85
G86
G87
G88
COLWYN BAY WIRELESS COLLEGE
G89
G90
G91
G92
WORCESTER
G93
G94
G95
G96
A T C
S C
C L B
G97
G98
G99
G100
CM

## F. Institutional Associations & Clubs

Social and representative bodies catering for membership needs.

**G.101** Meridian Lodge (Masonic)

**G.102** York Lodge (Masonic)

**G.103** Reform Club

**G.104** Ladies' Carlton Club

**G.105** City of London Club

**G.106** Cavendish Club

**G.107** Oxford and Cambridge Club

**G.108** Marylebone Cricket Club (law administering body)

**G.109** Cruising Association

**G.110** Shipping Federation

**G.111** Old Rugbeians

**G.112** Old Haileyburians Society

**G.113** Senior Golfers' Society

**G.114** Law Society

**G.115** National Fire Brigade Association

**G.116** Corps of Commissionaires

**G.117** British Legion

**G.118** Company of Merchants (Edinburgh)

**G.119** United Services Institution

**G.120** Soldiers' Sailors' and Airmen's (Families) Association

G101-G120
G101
G102
G103
G104
G105
G106
G107
G108
G109
G110
G111
G112
G113
G114
G115
G116
G117
G118
G119
G120
CM

## G. Sport & Leisure Pursuits Organisations

Generally catering for participants and supporters.

**G.121** Pembroke College Rowing Club

**G.122** British Motor Boat Club

**G.123** Royal Canoe Club

**G.124** St Peter's Boat Club

**G.125** Yare Sailing Club

**G.126** The Royal Cruising Club

**G.127** Royal Western Yacht Club

**G.128** Woodmen of Arden (archery)

**G.129** South Hants Cricket Club

**G.130** Pembroke Swimming Club

**G.131** Royal St George Golf Club

**G.132** Weston Super Mare Golf Club

**G.133** Glasgow University Athletics Club

**G.134** High Peak Harriers Hunt

**G.135** Celtic FC Supporters Club

**G.136** The Carnegie Club (outdoor pursuits)

**G.137** The British Button Society

**G.138** Trinity (Church) Choir Fareham

**G.139** Women's League of Health & Beauty

**G.140** Brighouse and Rastrick Band

G121-G130
BM BC
G121
G122
G123
G124
BOAT CLUB
SAILING CLUB
G125
G126
G127
G128
PEMBROKE SWIMMING CLUB
G129
G130
G131
G132
H.P.H.
CELTIC F.C.
SUPPORTERS ASSN.
G133
G134
G135
G136
CHOIR
W.L.H.B.
G137
G138
G139
G140
CM

## H. Commercial & Industrial Businesses

Essentially profit motivated concerns including manufacturers, retailers, and service providers.

**G.141** National Provincial Bank

**G.142** Westminster Bank Limited

**G.143** Sotheby's (Auctioneers)

**G.144** Harris and Dixon (ship brokers)

**G.145** Alliance Assurance

**G.146** Sun Alliance & London Insurance Group

**G.147** Dorchester Hotel

**G.148** Strand Palace Hotel

**G.149** Associated British Cinemas

**G.150** Joseph Cyril Bamford (plant)

**G.151** Esso Petroleum

**G.152** Shell Mex and British Petroleum

**G.153** Army & Navy Co-operative Society

**G.154** Imperial Chemical Industries

**G.155** WO and HO Wills (tobacco)

**G.156** Sutton and Sons (seedsmen)

**G.157** General Electric Company

**G.158** London & St Katharine Docks Company

**G.159** Carr (biscuits)

**G.160** Factory Guards (security provider)

G141-G160
WESTMINSTER BANK LIMITED
SOTHEBY'S
G141
G142
G143
G144
G145
G146
G147
G148
ABC
JCB
ESSO
SHELL-MEX & "BP" LTD
G149
G150
G151
G152
ICI
SUTTON & SONS
G153
G154
G155
G156
G.E.C
Carr
G157
G158
G159
G160
CM

# RECURRING DESIGN CONSTITUENTS

## Heraldic Designs

The motifs used on civilian uniform buttons vary widely in content and make-up, but where an organisation possesses heraldic arms these are often used as the insignia, particularly with issues by municipal and educational bodies. However, tunic buttons that display an organisation's complete armorial bearings, such as on the Mersey Tunnel Authority button (**G.35**), are not readily discernible on the "passing" uniform.

G35

G61

G24

Of better scale and more readily recognisable are heraldic compositions simplified to just a crest or shield. This is exemplified by the Liverpool City Bus Service and Ipswich Borough Council examples (**G.61** and **G.24**). Nevertheless, full heraldic arms can look very impressive and suggest importance. Interestingly, the one-time National Provincial Bank chose to display on its doormen's buttons its imposing full heraldic achievement, complete with double crest and supporters (**G.141**). By way of contrast, the Westminster Bank button (**G.142**) is just simply inscribed with the bank's title without any pictorial content. This comparatively austere design, however, implies a no-nonsense, business-like approach - which is possibly intended as a reflection of the manner of the bank's dealings.

G141

G142

G145

G146

The emblem on the Alliance Company's button **G.145**, upon this company's mergence within the Sun Alliance and London Insurance Group in 1965, became placed within the trefoil composition featured on button **G.146** to form a pleasing solution to the balancing problem of combining two company emblems with the armorial shield of another.

## Featured Dates, Locations, & "Image" Factors

G54

Besides its heraldic achievement, the button of the National Provincial Bank (**G.141**) also bears the date 1833. This refers to the year of the bank's formation, presumably to give assurance of reliability through long establishment. The date on the Royal Orphanage Wolverhampton button **G.54**, was apparently considered so important that it was centrally placed.

The buttons of a number of other long-founded bodies also include the date of origin. The Sotheby's button shown as **G.143** has "Founded 1744" beneath the firm's name, while on the Bancroft Hospital button (**G.58**) the date 1728 is recorded.

G143

G58

G144

G46

Sometimes an organisation's location, where this is not apparent from that body's title, is included within the button's design. The Harris & Dixon example (**G.144**) is an instance of this with "London" incorporated into the legend. The design of the West Midlands Fire Brigade's button (**G.46**), however, uniquely uses a map and shows the area

G156

that the brigade serves, as the button's motif. The firm Sutton & Sons, besides including its location "Reading" with a cartouche on its button (**G.156**), also boasts "The Queen's Seedsmen". Indeed many designs, especially those of commercial concerns, are intended to serve as miniature advertisements.

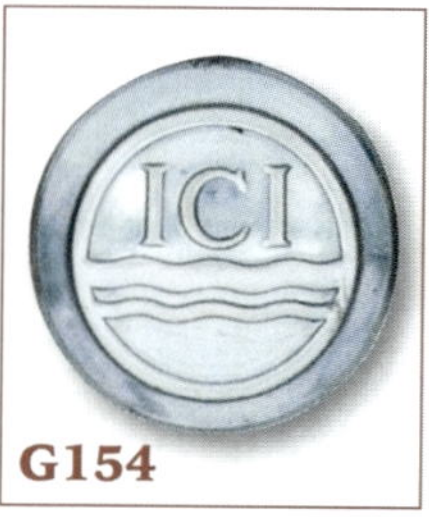

G154

G151

G16

G149

Trademarks, brand names, and logos generally reproduce well on button designs. Examples include the buttons of ICI (**G.154**), Esso (**G.151**), and the British Transport Docks Board (**G.16**). The company emblem used on buttons for the commissionaires of the Associated British Cinemas organisation (**G.149**) is very distinctive being Art Deco in style. As such it is fully consistent with the group's strong fashion image.

## Anchors & Crowns

G33

The Port of Bristol Authority button (**G.33**) has a roped rim, and this form of edging traditionally identifies maritime associations. It also displays an anchor. Anchor emblems are also much-featured on nautical-related buttons. The Seamen's Education Service button (**G.94**) is an example of this, as is the Royal Western Yacht Club button (**G.127**). The latter club's design also incorporates a representation of the royal crown to denote royal patronage.

G94

G127

G3

G9

G19

More often, though, the inclusion of the royal crown is to indicate "Crown Service" as on the uniform buttons worn by Coast Guards (**G.3**), His Majesty's Prison Service (**G.9**), and Her Majesty's Customs (**G.19**). The three different crown forms on these examples serve to illustrate the three styles of royal crown that occur as insignia. The first type is the St Edward's crown and was used as the royal emblem during the reigns of George IV to Queen Victoria inclusive. The second type is referred to as the Tudor-style crown and was used as insignia during the reigns of Edward VII to George VI inclusive. The third, high-arched, type is another version of the St Edward's crown and is unique to the reign of Queen Elizabeth II.

Besides royal crown forms, emblematic and heraldic coronets are used in some designs, respective examples being **G.79** and **G.126**.

G79

G126

The use of different royal crown versions can be a broad guide to dating the age of buttons. The exceptions are where a button bears the crown contemporary to that of the reigning monarch at the time when the organisation first received royal patronage instead of the crown respective to the current monarch to that of it actual time of issue. This situation applies to a number of organisations of early institution, including the Officers' Training Corps of Oxford University as proudly displayed on button **G.90**., while the crown on button **G.156** is indicative of royal appointment.

G90

G156

## Symbolic & Pictorial Representations

Many instances of symbolism occur on buttons serving to identify the roles of various organisations. A notable example is a design adopted by a number of Fire Brigades (including Anglesey as shown in **G.48**) made up of a fireman's helmet on two crossed axes. By association this very effectively shows the service of which the wearer is a member.

G48

G134

G121

Sports clubs' buttons often employ symbolism to represent their respective sports. The High Peak Harriers design features a running hare (**G.134**), while the Pembroke Rowing Club button displays crossed oars (**G.121**).

A stylised form of symbolism is used on the original British Airways Authorities button (**G.7**), this employs the very simple motif of parallel dashes, representative of parallel runways. Distinctively the buttons of the Royal Observer Corps (**G.11**) and the Northern Lighthouse Commission (**G.29**) both depict actual scenes. In the first case an observer is shown looking out to sea, apparently having ignited shoreline beacons; in the second, the picture is of a lighthouse and buoys in a turbulent sea.

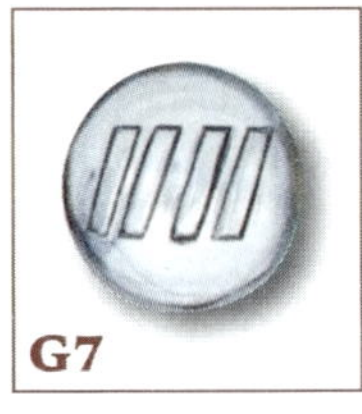
G7

G11

G29

The design on the buttons of the river Mersey Pilot Service crewmen (**G.40**) has classical associations. It

G40

G2

shows a figure representing the river watched over by the seated Roman personification Pax (Peace). A Roman classical figure is also used on the Bank of England button (**G.2**), in this case Britannia. This allegorical lady first appeared on English coins during the reign of Charles II, and she has graced many issues since. This particular button is not only appropriate to the Bank of England through the depiction of Britannia, but also from the fact that its form is very flat and coin-like.

G157

In the case of the General Electric Company button (**G.157**) symbolism appears in a manifest form. Besides its "electrical" motif the button itself is of polished copper, a metal widely used in the electrical engineering industry.

## Initials & Badges

Button motifs comprising the initials of the titles of concerns abound. The letters may be in simple succession, be represented in cipher form, or be within a monogram design. The characters themselves are also used in a great variety of font styles. Gothic lettering seems to have been favoured by long-established tradition bodies such as the Old Rugbeians Society, which displays the initials "ORS" (**G.111**), while the Maidenhead Voluntary Fire Brigade deployed its initials in a graceful calligraphic script (**G.47**). Both of these lettering styles contrast with the very plain capital letters "E.M.E.B." of the East Midlands Electricity Board's button (**G.27**).

G111

G47

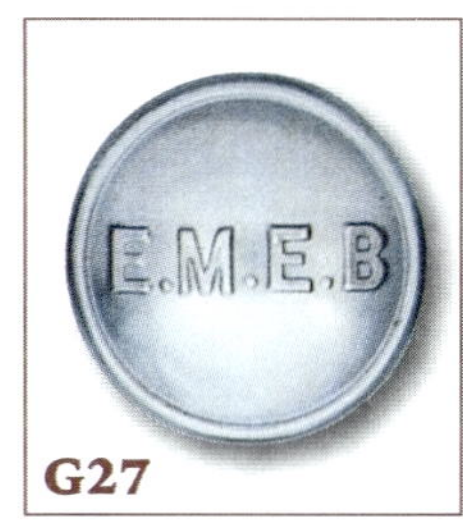

G27

G1

The General Post Office cipher "GPO" on its button illustrated as **G.1** is unnecessarily hard to read, but this was remedied with the Queen Elizabeth II issue.

G155

G50

The arrangement of the initials of the tobacco firm WD & WO Wills (**G.155**) well suits the button roundel setting and forms an interesting pattern. In the case of the London County Council Ambulance Service pre-1965 button (**G.50**) the initials are intertwined and overlapping whereby not even their order is apparent. This was typical of the designs of many concerns at the time when cipher-monograms were fashionable.

G12

G18

G117

G99

When the Air Raid Precautions Service (founded in 1938) became re-designated as the Civil Defence in 1941, the bland "ARP" initialled buttons (**G.12**) were replaced by ones bearing the initials "CD" (**G.18**). These new buttons were enhanced by the initials being surmounted by the royal crown, thus matching the tunic breast badge. Indeed, a number of organisations' button motifs are simply miniaturised reproductions of uniform badges where these are suitable. The British Legion and Church Lads' Brigade buttons are examples of this (**G.117** and **G.99**).

Chapter 2

# Differentiations & Updating

The great numbers and the variety of civilian uniform buttons produced have been enhanced over the years not only by the requirements of new organisations, but also through existing concerns producing revised and/or special designs.

The main factors causing changes and new designs arise from:-

Organisations developments within which necessitate amendments
Image presentation and fashion updating
Production costs considerations.

Consequently, the civilian uniform button scenario is ever expanding as a reflection of these circumstances.

To demonstrate this "fluid" situation, and to enable comparisons to be made in this chapter, 30 button examples have been presented and arranged into 12 groups (pairs, triples, and quads) with explanatory notes.

**D.1** Express Dairy early issue.

**D.2** Express Dairy later issue.

**D.3** Crosvill Motor Company early issue.

**D.4** Crosvill Motor Company later issue.

**D.5** Royal Automobile Club Edward VII issue.

**D.6** Royal Automobile Club later issue.

**D.7** 18th century livery button.

**D.8** 19th century livery button.

**D.9** Oakley Hunt field button.

**D.10** Oakley Hunt dress button.

**D.11** Livery coat button.

**D.12** Livery Highland dress button.

**D.13** Great Northern Railway general staff.

**D.14** Great Northern Railway senior staff.

## D1-D14

D1  D3  D5

D2 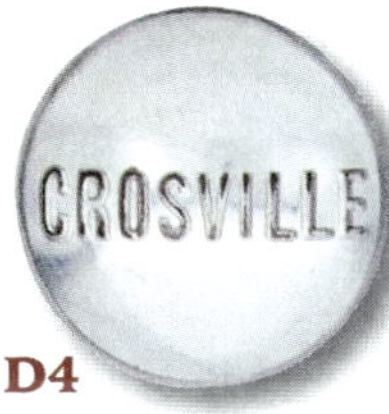 D4  D6

D7  D8

D9  D11  D13

D10 D12 D14

CM

**D.15** Somerset Constabulary pre-1967.

**D.16** Somerset Constabulary 1967-1974.

**D.17** Avon & Somerset Constabulary 1974-

**D.18** British Railways 1949 issue.

**D.19** British Railways 1964 issue.

**D.20** British Railways 1966 issue.

**D.21** British Railways enamelled issue (ceased 1994).

**D.22** Hertfordshire Ambulance Brigade.

**D.23** Hertfordshire Fire Brigade.

**D.24** Crown Premises Queen Victoria issue.

**D.25** Crown Premises King's Crown issue (a).

**D.26** Crown Premises King's Crown issue (b).

**D.27** Crown Premises Queen Elizabeth II issue.

**D.28** Birmingham and Dudley District Bank (established 1836)

**D.29** Midlands Bank 1923 issue.

**D.30** Midlands Bank 1950 issue.

## D15-D30

D15

D16

D17

D18

D19

D20

D21

D22

D23

D24

D25

D26

D27

D28

D29

D30

CM

The names of many employing concerns are often only identified on buttons by an emblem or inscription. Other concerns, however, also indicate the particular service on which their employees are engaged. For example, the Corporation of Portsmouth button (**G.68**) besides its name identifies the service provided ie "Tramways," in the legend. Some inscriptions can be very specific, whereby an actual post is "spelt out", as in the case of the Swansea Attendance Officer (**G.38**).

G68

G38

G70

A practice with certain companies has been to issue differing buttons to distinguish between senior and lesser uniformed members of staff; in particular this applies to railway companies. In the case of the London Midland & Scottish Railway (**G.70**), rank distinction was made by issuing gilt finish buttons for senior employees and white metal ones to others. This approach came to be adopted in turn by British Railways.

D13

D14

In the case of the Great Northern Railway, two quite different designs were issued which differed in quality also: gilt for high echelon staff, **(D.14)** and brass for the remainder (**D.13)**.

G63

Another instance of distinction is the use of contrasting materials as used on Leeds City Transport uniforms. Chromium plated buttons are provided for the coats of conductors and drivers (**G.63**), while inspectors have buttons of black composition. The design of the buttons is otherwise identical.

Different materials do not, however, necessarily indicate different appointments, as exemplified by many police forces' uniforms. Buttons made of black composition are used on topcoats and mackintoshes, while those on tunics are chromium plated - regardless of the rank of the wearer.

Another reason for variation can be because an organisation chose to have buttons for different occasions. Many Hunt Clubs, besides having a field pattern, also have a special version for dress occasions. Very often the two types are alike apart from their quality, and this is so in the case of the Oakley Hunt button. The field button is of a one piece struck form, with an embossed marquis' coronet above the letter "0", set on a ribbed field, while, the dress version is a high domed gilt two-piece type with the coronet and an ornate "0" mounted upon it (see **D.9** and **D.10**).

D9

D10

Examples of varying qualities of buttons abound amongst Royal Court issues to suit the different "levels" of occasions (as demonstrated in Chapter 4).

Another circumstance giving rise to distinction occurs with certain livery buttons, as noted in Chapter 3, whereby blackened finish pieces were sometimes substituted during the period of mourning following the death of the "master".

G51

D22

D23

Many Municipal Authorities responsible for more than one uniformed service, have made no distinction between the issued buttons. Notably, Kingston-upon-Hull at one time provided the same button design to its Police, Ambulance, and Transport services personnel (**G.51**).

In the case of the County of Hertfordshire, it issued separate buttons to its Fire and Ambulance Brigades, but the subtle one-initial difference is easily overlooked (compare **D.22** and **D.23**).

The primary cause for organisations changing their button designs is often "up-dating". Image presentation and corporate identity have increased in importance with the perceived need to be "with it". The general trend, particularly in respect of emblems used, is for designs to be very simple but at the same time readily identifiable. The examples illustrated of earlier and later patterns of the Express Dairy(**D.1** and **D.2**), Crosville Motor Services (**D.3** and **D.4**) and the R.A.C. buttons (**D.5** and **D.6**) demonstrate this well.

D1

D3

D5

D2

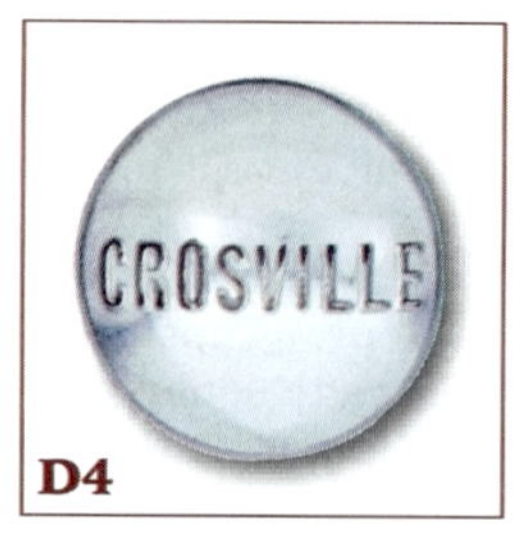

D4

D6

**D15**

**D16**

**D17**

However, to simplify is not necessarily to improve. An instance of unsatisfactory replacement in respect of distinction is surely that of the Somerset Constabulary "experience". Regrettably, the popular heraldic dragon (**D.15**) came to be superseded by a crown and legend pattern (**D.16**) common to that used by many other police forces. When the Somerset force was merged with Avon, matters became compounded, as the new button comprises a motif of a crown alone (**D.17**).

This crown design is being widely adopted by many forces including use by traffic wardens, although it has been claimed that diminishing distinction leads to diminished allegiance.

**D7**

**D8**

It is interesting to compare the two livery buttons **D.7** and **D.8**, which bear the same crest. The large one was made in the 18th century, and its device is hand engraved upon the flat solid silver flan. The second button was made in the 19th century. It is of silver plate on copper, of concave one-piece form, and has its crest in raised relief. These two buttons serve as good examples of both style and make-up of their respective times.

D28

D29

D30

When company amalgamations occur and heraldic arms are affected, button designs can record this. The button of the amalgamated Birmingham and Dudley & District banks is an example (**D.28**). The respective shields are displayed in an adjoining arms relationship.

The shields of the Midland Bank of 1923, comprising the arms of the Central bank of London (acquired in 1891) and the Midland Bank (founded 1836) are displayed as co-joined together (**D.29**). However, the Midland Bank button design of 1950 shows the two constituent arms compounded into a one shield composition (**D.30**).

D18

D19

D20

D21

British Railways buttons **D.18**, **D.19**, **D.20** and **D.21** issued between 1949 and 1994, purely record logo changes in pursuance of keeping abreast of fashion trends. All examples were made of both gilt and white metal/ chromium plated finishes, to provide for distinction between senior and lesser staff appointments.

D24

D25

D26

D27

Buttons **D.24**, **D.25**, **D.26** and **D.27** were worn by uniformed staff at Crown premises. They serve to clearly show the Queen Victoria Crown, King's Crown (issue (a) and (b)), and Elizabeth II Crown types. The difference between the two King's Crown representations is due to versions being made by different makers. The first type shown occurred mostly during Edward VII's reign.

Different button "shape forms" for different costumes are unusual but the two livery buttons **D.11** and **D.12** (bearing the Wyvern crest of the Wills family and the motto "As God wills") cater for normal dress and Highland dress respectively.

D11

D12

## HERALDIC CREST LIVERY BUTTONS

The components that make up an Heraldic design achievement normally comprise six basic parts:-

**1.** The Crest

**2.** The Wreath
(or crest "mount" forms)

**3.** The Helmet

**4.** The Mantling
(symbolic cape)

**5.** The Shield
(Coat of Arms)

**6.** The motto.

*Lion sejant guardant erect crest form, wreath mounted.*

To these however may be added by reason of rank or honour:-

**A.** Supporters
(flanking figures)

**B.** A Compartment
(base)

**C.** A Coronet of Rank

**D.** An insignia of Chivalry

Whilst a Crest cannot, in heraldic terms, exist without there being a Coat of Arms (for it is only part of an achievement), Crests nevertheless came to be widely used as the designs featured upon most household livery buttons.

Lion crest forms occur most of all, being much favoured as symbols of strength.

Chapter 3

# Livery Buttons

In the 15th century "livery" referred to the food and keep provided to a servant by his employer. For recognition purposes, livered servants came to be issued with badges to wear depicting their masters' insignia, which were usually of heraldic designs. From this practice, clothing of individual "cut" and cloth for certain servants (notably footmen) was required to be worn. This not only served as a distinctive uniform, but also to reflect the prestige of the employer. This led to heraldic insignia, by the 18th century, being "transferred" from badges to buttons. Thereafter such buttons became known as livery buttons.

Livery buttons of the late 18th century were large as **D.7** (about 36mm in diameter), of one-piece construction, and their design was hand engraved. By the early 19th century and thereafter, livery buttons were reduced in size to some 25mm in diameter, with the buttons used on coachmen's topcoats generally being larger, and waistcoat buttons much smaller.

Two-piece buttons came to be made as an option. These were more suitable for high dome designs, both one and two piece buttons being manufactured by die striking. Most designs consisted of family heraldic crests only, whose simplicity (see **L.2**) suited the small scale of buttons.

L2

L1

L15

L26

However, some buttons also bear family mottoes as **L.1**, and/or the arms as **L.15**. Double crests also occur in the event of a second surname and armorial achievement being assumed through marriage (see **L.26**).

L39

L40

Women's livery buttons are easily recognised as such, because their designs are restricted to lozenge shaped shields, either of a simple diamond shape or of a curvilinear form. However, without the lead of a crest or motto etc, it can be very difficult to trace the owner's name (see **L.39** and **L.40**).

In the case of peers' buttons the status is indicated by the respective coronet - duke, marquis, earl, viscount or baron - being included and placed above the crest displayed on each button (see page 45). In respect of baronets' buttons, a representation of the Hand of Ulster badge is included (as **L.58**, **L.59** and **L.60**).

L58

L59

L60

Peer's livery buttons provided for coachmen, being usually extra large, gave scope for displays of full achievements, and appear grand indeed as illustrated on page 53.

The use of livery buttons came to a peak in Edwardian times, their use thereafter dropping away as a reflection of the changes that were taking place in contemporary society.

Livery buttons were rarely made of solid silver; most were of Sheffield plate (silver bonded to copper). This was extensively used, (being said to mark clothing less,), even after 1850 when electro-plating was widespread. Those buttons required to appear "gold" were sometimes of brass but more often given a gilt finish. The choice of silver or gold was not arbitrary, but was determined by the principle tincture of the respective heraldic achievement. A black finish to buttons was fashionable in the event of mourning, and was often achieved by chemical treatment or by coating.

*Naval crown*

*Palisado crown*

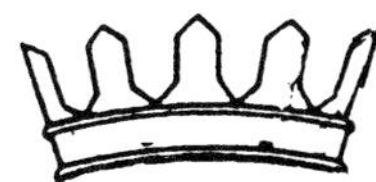

*Crown vallary*

*Chapeau*

*Ducal or crest coronet*

*Mural crown*

*Baron's coronet*

*Viscount's coronet*

*Earl's coronet*

*Marquess's coronet*

*Duke's coronet*

**Crowns and Coronets used with Livery Buttons**

## Examples Of Household Family Livery Buttons

FAMILY NAMES

**L.1** Adair

**L.2** Ashton

**L.3** Atkinson

**L.4** Austen

**L.5** Baddelay

**L.6** Barrow

**L.7** Beachaump

**L.8** Birch

**L.9** Borlase

**L.10** Brodie

**L.11** Rev. Churchman

**L.12** Dallas

**L.13** Rev. Danbuz

**L.14** Eyre

**L.15** Foster

**L.16** Fox

**L.17** Greenwood

**L.18** Halliday

**L.19** Harp

**L.20** Heathcote

L1-L20
L1
L2
L3
L4
L5
L6
L7
L8
UNITE
L9
L10
L11
L12
L13
L14
L15
L16
L17
L18
L19
L20
CM

**L.21** Hopper

**L.22** Hunter

**L.23** Leith

**L.24** Le Mesurier

**L.25** Marchmont

**L.26** Meynell-Ingram

**L.27** Middleton

**L.28** Mills

**L.29** Niven

**L.30** Phillot

**L.31** Polwhele

**L.32** Adml. Reynolds

**L.33** Riddell

**L.34** Rev. Roberts

**L.35** Samuels

**L.36** Spry

**L.37** Capt. Tyler

**L.38** Wilkinson

**L.39** Unidentified woman's arms (widow)

**L.40** Unidentified woman's arms (widow)

L21-L40
L21
L22
L23
L24
L25
L26
L27
L28
L29
L30
L31
L32
L33
L34
L35
L36
L37
L38
L39
L40
CM

## LIVERY BUTTONS OF BISHOPS, PEERS & BARONETS

**L.41** Lord John Beresford Archbishop of Armagh

**L.42** Bishop of Kilmore

**L.43** Duke of Atholl

**L.44** Duke of Bedford

**L.45** Duke of Fife

**L.46** Duke of Richmond

**L.47** Marquis of Camden

**L.48** Marquis of Northampton

**L.49** Earl of Longsdale

**L.50** Earl of Romsey

**L.51** Earl of Scarborough

**L.52** Viscount Boyne

**L.53** Viscount Hill

**L.54** Baron Chesham

**L.55** Baron Hastings

**L.56** Baron Waldergove

**L.57** An unidentified baroness

**L.58** Sir Theodore Brinkman, Bart

**L.59** Sir Robert Buxton, Bart

**L.60** Sir Charles Jepson-Norris, Bart

L41-L60
L41
L42
L43
L44
L45
R
L46
L47
L48
L49
ORA ET LABORA
L50
L51
NEC TIMEO NEC SPERNO
L52
L53
L54
SUSTENTE · TENAX
L55
NIL NISI CRUCE
L56
L57
PERSEVERANDO
L58
L59
L60
CM

## LIVERY BUTTONS OF PEERS
(A selection of particularly distinctive designs)

**L.61** Duke of Norfolk

**L.62** Duke of Hamilton

**L.63** Marquis of Abergavenny

**L.64** Marquis of Crewe

**L.65** Marquis of Lothian

**L.66** Earl of Bathurst

**L.67** Earl of Lodesborough

**L.68** Earl of Dundonald

**L.69** Baron Lyons

**L.70** Baron Seagrave

**L.71** Baron Rothschild

**L.72** Baron Petre

The size of many of these buttons suggests that they were worn by coachmen.

L61-L72
L61
THROUGH
L62
L63
L64
L65
L66
L67
L68
L69
DIEU NOUS AVEC
L70
L71
L72
CM

*Full state postilion jacket embellished with 47 buttons*

Chapter 4

# Royal Court Buttons

The term Royal Court buttons is used to describe "uniform" buttons required to be worn on royal occasions by members of the Royal Household and officers in attendance, together with the buttons worn on the liveries of certain domestic staff engaged at Royal premises. Regulation and practice determine the "level" of attire - ranging from modest to ceremonial splendour - according to the nature and importance of each particular occasion. The costume worn by Royalty, Royal Household members, dignitaries, and ceremonial post holders, is referred to as "dress", and is classified as being undress (ie day to day wear), evening dress, levee dress (ie for receptions), or full dress, which is worn on the most important and ceremonial occasions.

The attire worn by uniformed employee domestic staff personnel is known as "livery", and this includes footmen, coachmen, and pages. The different liveries are established by tradition, and this applies to the button designs too.

These liveries, and in some cases the buttons as well, can vary according to seniority and place of employment besides that of occasion. Liveries include normal daily dress, scarlet livery, semi-state livery, or full state livery. However, there are not necessarily different liveries for all different "levels" of occasions. The system of regulated dress is complex indeed!

The designs on the livery buttons used, comprise mainly crowns, royal ciphers and heraldic designs. Over the years these have needed updating to bring them in line not only with new sovereign ascendances, but also to account for marriages and children as they grow up to have their own households. All royal family members who undertake public engagements have households of their own. These include full-time personnel and others who from time to time assist with public duties. But, of course, it is the Queen's Household that is really extensive, with officials and domestics numbering some 650 persons.

## ROYAL COURT BUTTONS

**R.1**, **R.2**, **R.3**, **R.4**, **R.5**, and **R.6** Officers at Arms to Queen Victoria, Edward VII, George V, Edward VIII, George VI, and Queen Elizabeth II. Also The Earl Marshall and The Master of the Horse.

(NB This set of buttons displays the royal ciphers and respective crowns, and may serve to date other buttons upon which these emblems occur).

**R.7**, **R.8**, **R.9**, and **R.10** H.M. Lieutenants of Counties for England, Scotland, Wales, and Northern Ireland respectively.

**R.11** Lieutenant of the City of London.

**R.12** Lord Lieutenant of Northern Ireland.

**R.13** City Marshall.

**R.14** Deputy-Lieutenant of County.

**R.15**, **R.16** and **R.17** H.M. Household evening dress.

## R1-R17

R1

R2

R3

R4

R5

R6

R7

R8

R9

R10

R11

R12

R13

R14

R15

R16

R17

CM

**R.18**, **R.19**, and **R.20** H.M. Royal Household, full dress (note the different crowns).

**R.21** (alternative cipher type to R.22), **R.22**, **R.23** and **R.24** H.M. Equerries and Aides-de-Camp, former Regular Army officers.

**R.25** and **R.26** H.M. Equerries and Aides-de-Camp, former Territorial Army officers.

**R.27** and **R.28** Equerries to the Prince of Wales.

**R.29**, **R.30** and **R.31** H.M. Royal Household, levee dress.

**R.32** and **R.33** Windsor uniform.

**R.34** Royal Academicians.

**R.35** Trinity House Elder Brothers.

## R18-R35

R18

R19

R20

R21

R22

R23

R24

R25

R26

R27

R28

R29

R30

R31

R32

R33

R34

R35

CM

**R.36** and **R.37** Yeomen of the Guard.

**R.38** and **R.39** Sovereign's Body Guard of the Yeomen of the Guard (officers).

**R.40** and **R.41** H.M. Body Guard of the Honourable Corps of Gentlemen-at-Arms.

**R.42** Military Knights of Windsor.

**R.43**, **R.44**, **R.45**, and **R.46** The Sovereign's Body Guard for Scotland. (NB R.43 and R.44 relate to George IV and William IV).

**R.47** Governors-General.

**R.48** Consular Service, full and levee dress.

**R.49** Consular Service, undress.

**R.50** Pages of Honour.

**R.51** H.M. Marshalmen

**R.52**, **R.53**, and **R.54** H.M. Swankeeper, Bargemaster, and Watermen.

R36-R54

R36  R37  R38  R39

R40  R41  R42

R43 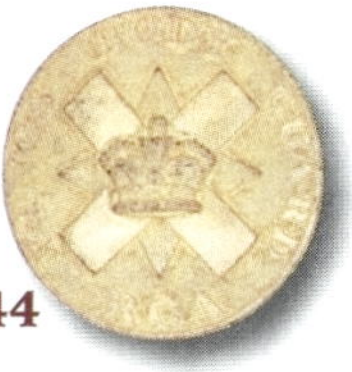 R44  R45  R46

R47  R48  R49  R50

R51  R52  R53  R54

CM

**R.55** Staff to Prince Leopold.

**R.56** Postilion to H.M. the King.

**R.57** Footman to Queen Mary (scarlet livery).

**R.58** Staff to Queen Elizabeth the Queen Mother.

**R.59** Staff to Duke & Duchess of Argyll.

**R.60** Staff to Albert & Alexandria, Prince and Princess of Wales.

**R.61** Staff to George & Mary, Prince and Princess of Wales.

**R.62** Coachmen to Alfred & Marie, Duke and Duchess of Edinburgh.

**R.63** Coachmen to H.M. the King.

**R.64** Pages of Chamber, Backstairs and Presence.

**R.65** and **R.66** Carriage Footmen.

**R.67** Attendants Westminster Palace.

**R.68** and **R.69** Scarlet Livery Footmen.

**R.70** and **R.71** General Palace Staff.

R55-R71
R55
R56
R57
R58
R59
R60
R61
R62
R63
R64
R65
R66
R67
R68
R69
R70
R71
CM

## A SELECTION OF ROYAL APPOINTMENTS WITH COURT & CEREMONIAL DRESS

The duties are often not readily known in respect of the many and various household members, appointed officers, and domestic staff required to wear dress uniforms or livery equipped with special buttons. Accordingly, outline descriptions of a selection of appointments are set out below to enable readers to relate these to the respective buttons.

R1

R2

R3

R4

R5

R6

### Earl Marshall of England

(**R.1**, **R.2**, **R.3**, **R.4**, **R.5** and **R.6**)

A Great Officer of State responsible for matters of arms, dignities, precedence and honour. He is overall organiser of State Ceremonies.

### The Master of the Horse

(**R.1**, **R.2**, **R.3**, **R.4**, **R.5** and **R.6**)

Great Officer of HM Household, in charge of the Royal stables and organiser of all state processions.

### Officers of Arms

(**R.1**, **R.2**, **R.3**, **R.4**, **R.5** and **R.6**)

Concerned with grants of armorial bearings and such heraldic matters, and state processions participation.

R13

R32

R33

## City Marshall

(**R.13**)

Ceremonial appointment, this official was formerly responsible for keeping order in the streets of London.

## Windsor Uniform

(**R.32** and **R.33**)

Court dress for wear at Windsor Castle only by members of the Royal family, and Privileged Household members.

R40

R41

R42

## Honourable Corps of Gentlemen-at-Arms

(**R.40** and **R.41**)

Senior Royal bodyguard acting as escort in royal processions and on guard at Westminster Abbey during coronations.

## Military Knights of Windsor

(**R.42**)

Body of privileged former army officers receiving allowances and free accommodation at Windsor Castle where they help at ceremonies.

R43

R44

R45

R46

## Gentlemen of the Royal Company of Archers

(**R.43**, **R.44**, **R.45**, and **R.46**)

Serves as the monarch's ceremonial bodyguard when the sovereign visits Scotland.

R50

R51

## Pages of Honour

(**R.50**)

Ceremonial appointments, selected from sons of the sovereign's friends and Household members, to carry the Queen's train.

## H.M. Marshalmen

(**R.51**)

A ceremonial appointment with duties that notably include presence at the Changing of the Guard.

R52

R53

R54

## H.M. Royal Swan Keeper
(**R.52**, **R.53**, and **R.54)**

Keeper of the sovereign's swans and responsible for the arrangement of the "swan upping" ceremony.

## H.M. Watermen
(**R.52**, **R.53**, and **R.54**)

Attend upon those guests of the sovereign who travel on the River Thames, and serve as box men on the State Opening of Parliament

## H.M. Bargemaster
(**R.52**, **R.53**, and **R.54**)

Although the Royal State Barge is no longer used, this officer still takes part in state processions.

R64

## Page of the Chamber, Pages of the Backstairs, & Pages of the Presence
(**R.64**)

These post holders are all members of the Master of the Household's staff.

BY APPOINTMENT

# ESTABLISHED 1677

*(Facsimile of an Old Plate in use towards the end of the Seventeenth Century.)*

MANUFACTURERS TO THE TRADE OF
BUTTONS,
BADGES, ACCOUTREMENTS,
CAPS AND MEDALS

# FIRMIN & SONS LTD.

8, CORK ST., LONDON, W.1

*Telephone:* Regent 1815. *Telegrams:* Firmin, Piccy, London.

*Advertisement from "Dress & Insignia Worn at Court 1937"*

# Chapter 5

# Button Making & Backmarks

*This chapter has been compiled in collaboration with Keith Riddle of the BMBC (The British Military Button Company).*

## Button Making

In Victorian times most metal uniform buttons, both civilian and military, were struck in base metals of brass, white metal and copper alloys such as gilding metal. Buttons with a higher quality finish were gold or silver-plated and in some instances even made in solid silver. Dyed pressed horn was used for the black horn buttons. However, chromium-plated white metal buttons that needed no polishing came into general use in the 1930s, with a later innovation of buttons made from pre-chromium plated brass. Anodised aluminium (commonly but erroneously referred to as "Staybrite", as this is really the registered name for a form of stainless steel), was introduced in the 1950s. Another innovation has been metal-coated plastic buttons with a shiny metal surface finish. Black horn has been successively replaced by vulcanite and a black plastic composition (polypropylene). Fortunately, the traditional finishes are still in production.

Coloured enamelling is uncommon on uniform buttons but in the past the Women's League of Health and Beauty issued a number in different colours (see **G.139**), while the Weston Super Mare Golf Club button has the enamelling limited to just the flag emblem (see **G.132**).

G139

G132

The manner of making buttons has changed little from that of 150 years ago; sometimes different and more sophisticated machinery is used, but the craft skills are still required at each different stage.

Descriptions of buttons often include the expressions one-piece and two-piece. The meaning of terms such as these are made clear by the annotated diagrams on page 71, while page 70 provides a description of how two-piece buttons are made.

## The Manufacture Of Two-Piece Buttons

**The Die** - A large scale pattern illustrating the proposed button design is used to transfer the required design by cutting this into the face of a steel die by pantograph in mirror image and to the diameter of the finished button.

**Lead Impression** - A lead slug is stamped into the die enabling examination of the quality of the button design.

**Hardening** - The die, when approved, is then heated and immersed in oil to harden it.

**Shells** - These are the prepared plain dome pieces formed on a power press ready to receive the design.

**Stamping** - a shell is placed between an upper and lower die, which when brought together in a drop stamp or stamping machine embosses the design onto the face of the button shell.

**Backs** - These are the disc pieces to which shanks are fitted and fused before "closing". If the backs are required to have any backmarks (ie the manufacturer's name), this is done as one operation when making the backs.

**Closing** - The method by which a front shell is joined to its back disc at the rim edge. This is effected either by machine crimping (termed "pressed") or else by setting the back disc into a perimeter rebate in the shell, and spinning on a lathe to form a fused smooth joint termed "spun".

**Mounts** - These separate die stampings or castings have pegs projecting from their backs which pass through pre-drilled holes in the shells. The pegs are then turned over inside the shells to secure the mount. This operation is carried out before "closing".

**Plating** - Shells if required, may be plated with a surface finish such as gilt, silver plate, chrome etc, by an electrolytic process also carried out before "closing". Button fronts may also be burnished to provide polished highlights on the matt field or polished all over on a polishing mop.

## BUTTON CONSTRUCTION & SHANK TYPES

Flat one-piece button fitted with a footed "M" shank.

Convex one-piece button fitted with a half loop shank (open back type).

Closed "solid" assembly fitted with an un-footed shank.

Spun two-piece button with set-back shell and inset back, fitted with a swan neck footed shank and mounted emblem.

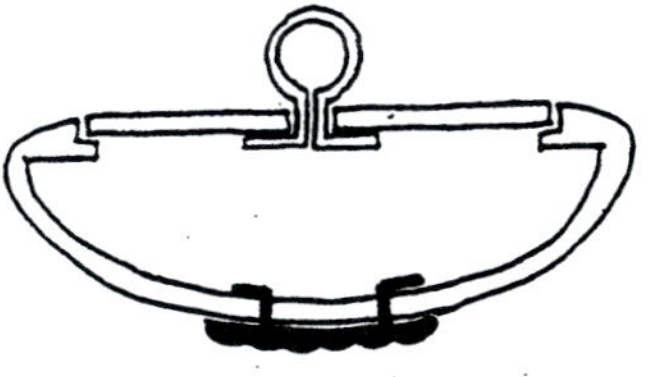

Pressed back two-piece button fitted with a drop shank assembly.

## Backmarks

The term "backmarks" refers to the inscriptions (usually in legend form) and/or trade marks on the back of buttons. These are formed as either embossed or impressed lettering at the time of a button's manufacture, being integral to the dies used.

Backmarks identify the manufacturer's name (and sometimes address too), or the supplier's/tailor's identity. Backmarks can also refer to the quality assurance of the button itself.

The selection of backmarks on page 75 **Column I** consists of examples of quality references, while **Column II** and **Column III** list notable manufacturers. It should be noted, however, that dates given on page 74 apply to the period of use of the particular backmark, and not necessarily the duration of the existence of the respective button making firm. Further it should be borne in mind that abbreviated inscriptions are usual on small buttons (such as those for cuffs and waistcoats), and this adds to the difficulties of dating.

**Column IV** is made up of examples of suppliers and tailors who have arranged to have their identities inscribed on the pieces ordered from co-operative manufacturers. The different backmark inscriptions can serve as an aid to dating the time of manufacture of a button, where supporting information is available for reference. Interestingly, the varying backmark inscriptions often record developments affecting makers in the way of name changes (often due to take-overs), and to changes to addresses. However, research can prove to be no light undertaking! It usually involves scrutiny of, in particular, old trade and street directories. As an indication of the complexity of this, on page 73 are listed the backmarks accredited to the two most productive button makers Firmin and Gaunt. This information is an extract from an article compiled by Roger Millward, published in the British Button Society's journal *Button Lines*, Issue 106 March 2001.

S. FIRMIN STRAND - 1771-1780
FIRMIN & WESTALL - 1794-1812
FIRMIN & LANGDALE - 1811-1821
FIRMIN STRAND LONDON - c1825
P & S FIRMIN - 1837
FIRMIN & SONS 153 STRAND - 1875
FIRMIN & SONS, 153 STRAND LONDON - 1875
FIRMIN & SONS 153 STRAND &
13 CONDUIT ST LONDON - 1852-1875
FIRMIN & SONS, 13 CONDUIT ST. LONDON
FIRMIN & SONS LD 153 STRAND LONDON - 1876-1894
FIRMIN & SONS LD 135 STRAND LONDON (error) -
1876-1894
FIRMIN & SONS LD 153 STRAND,
47 WARWICK ST LONDON - 1880-1894
FIRMINS 47 WARWICK STREET W LONDON - 1879-1904
FIRMIN & SONS LTD, 6 WARWICK ST.,
REGENT ST LONDON
FIRMIN & SONS LD ST MARTINS LANE
LONDON - 1895-1915
FIRMIN & SONS LD 108 ST MARTINS LANE
LONDON - 1895-1915
FIRMIN & SONS LD LONDON - early 20th century
FIRMIN & SONS LTD LONDON - early 20th century
FIRMINS LTD LONDON - 20th century
FIRMIN & SONS LTD LONDON PATENT 2346 - 1884-?
FIRMIN & SONS LONDON - late 19th century
FIRMIN LONDON - mid 20th century
FIRMIN ENGLAND - mid 20th century
FIRMIN LONDON & BIRMINGHAM - 1882-
FIRMIN'S LONDON & B'HAM - 1882-
FIRMIN LTD LONDON & BIRMINGHAM - 1882-
FIRMIN & SONS LD BIRMINGHAM - 1882-
FIRMIN & SONS LD HALESOWEN - 1882-

J R GAUNT & SON LONDON - 1884-1899 but also used well after this date
J R GAUNT & SON LTD LONDON - 1899-1991
J R GAUNT & SON LTD LONDON ENG - 1899-1991
J R GAUNT & SON LTD LONDON ENGLD - 1899-1991
J R GAUNT & SON LTD LONDON ENGLAND - 1899-1991
J R GAUNT & SON LTD LATE JENNENS LONDON -
1940-1948
J R GAUNT & SONS MONTREAL -
J R GAUNT & SON LTD MONTREAL - c1914-c1939
J R GAUNT & SON LTD MONTREAL
MADE IN ENGLAND - c1901-1939?
J R GAUNT & SON BIRMINGHAM - 1870-1973
GAUNT LONDON - 1950s/60s onwards
GAUNT LONDON ENG - 1950s/60s onwards

## BACKMARKS

**Column I**

**B.1** Extra Superfine - Best Quality

**B.2** Treble Gilt - Standard

**B.3** Warranted Standard

**B.4** Rivet' & Solderd

**Columns II & III**

**B.5** E. ARMFIELD & CO. BIRMINGHAM (1911-1975)

**B.6** BOGGETT & REYNOLDS. ST MARTINS LANE. LONDON (1843-1861)

**B.7** R BUSHBY. ST MARTINS LANE (1806-1824)

**B.8** BUTTONS LTD BIRMINGHAM (1907-1959). Note the crossed swords Trade Mark.

**B.9** FIRMIN & SON. 153 STRAND. LONDON (1876-1894)

**B.10** JENNENS & CO. LONDON (1912-1924). Note the Prince of Wales' Feathers Trade Mark.

**B.11** PITT & CO. 31 MADDOX ST. LONDON. W (1895-1973)

**B.12** J.W. REYNOLDS & CO. 50 ST MARTINS LANE LONDON (1861-1870)

**B.13** SHERLOCK & CO. COVENT GARDEN. LONDON (1845-1880)

**B.14** WYON. 287 REGENT ST LONDON. ENGRAVER TO HER MAJESTY (c1838-c1842)

**Column IV**

**B.15** ARMY & NAVY CO (1918-1952)

**B.16** S.W. SILVER & CO. CLOTHIERS. LONDON (c1865-1875)

**B.17** SIMPSON & SON. 61 SOUTH AUDLEY ST. LONDON (1861-1885)

**B.18** HAWKES & CO. PICCADILLY. LONDON (1853-1912)

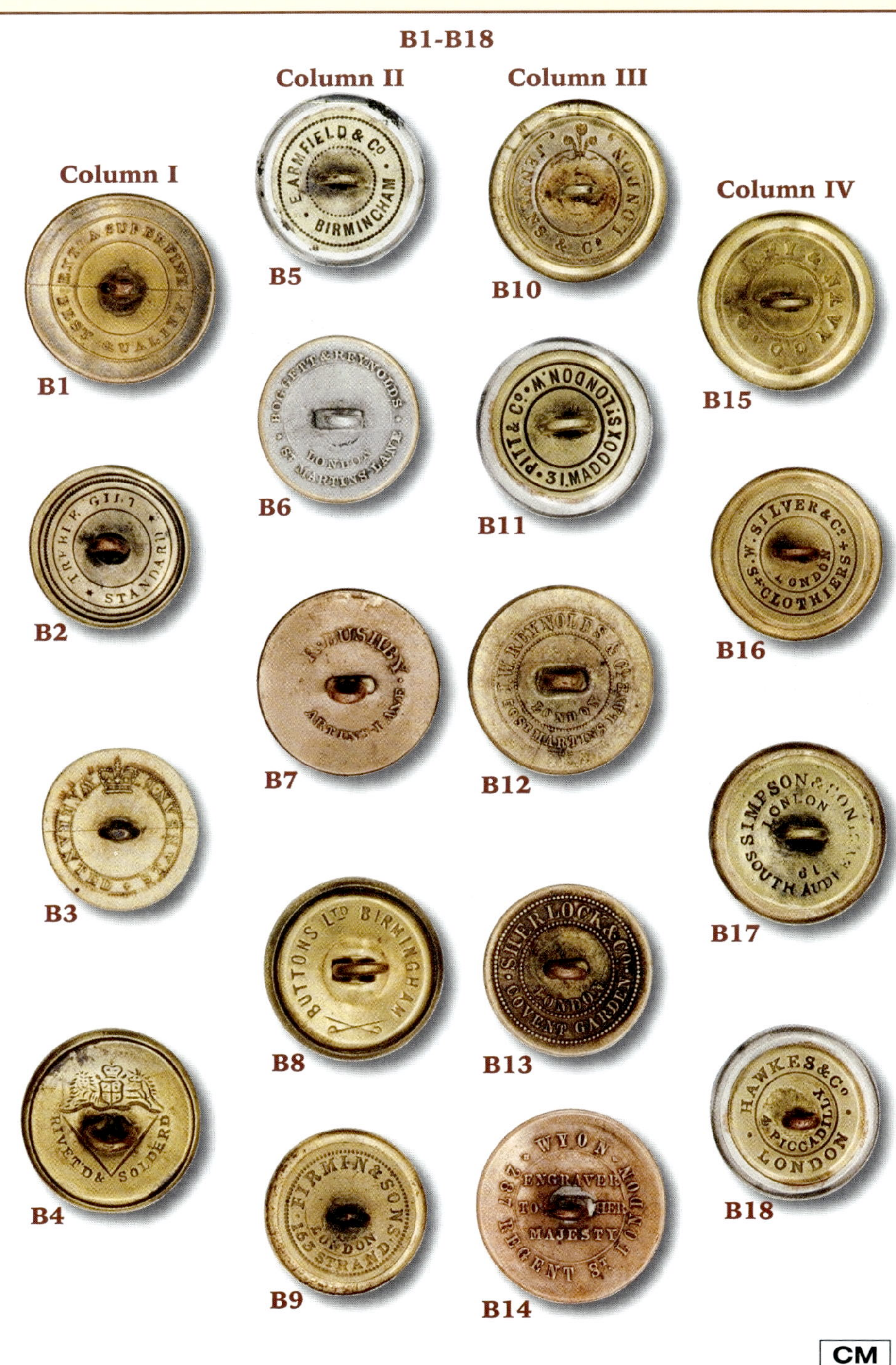
B1-B18
Column I
Column II
Column III
Column IV
EXTRA SUPERFINE BEST QUALITY
B1
STANDARD
B2
B3
RIVETD & SOLDERD
B4
E. ARMFIELD & Co BIRMINGHAM
B5
BOGGETT & REYNOLDS LONDON St MARTINS LANE
B6
B7
BUTTONS LTD BIRMINGHAM
B8
FIRMIN & SONS LONDON 153 STRAND
B9
JENNENS & Co LONDON
B10
PITT & Co. 31. MADDOX St LONDON. W.
B11
B12
SHERLOCK & CO. LONDON COVENT GARDEN
B13
WYON ENGRAVER TO HER MAJESTY 287 REGENT St LONDON
B14
B15
S. W. SILVER & Co LONDON CLOTHIERS
B16
SIMPSON & SON LONDON
B17
HAWKES & Co PICCADILLY LONDON
B18
CM

Fig.1. Fig.2. Fig.3. Fig.4. Fig.5. Fig.6. Fig.7. Fig.8.

## Some Interesting & Unusual Buttons

**Figs.1., 2., & 3.** Scottish Pipers' Highland Dress buttons, lozenge shaped.

**Fig.4.** A special Civic Occasions button of the City of Litchfield, which reproduces the design of the City Seal.

**Fig.5.** A hunt servant's button bearing the date 1910-11. Its legend identifies the hunt club and its one time kennels location (ie the Wentworth Pack of Lord Fitzwilliams).

**Fig.6.** A Lloyds Bank button with a circlet made up of alternating bees and beehives presumably reflecting Cockney slang for money ("bees and honey").

**Fig.7.** A button with the words "Trade Mark" below the representation of a fountain, but otherwise having no identification.

**Fig.8.** A button bearing the royal cipher of King William IV, recovered by a metal detectorist.

# Chapter 6

# Collecting Themes

The button examples contained in the preceding pages to this chapter, while intended to provide an overall appreciation of the types of civilian uniform buttons that have come into being, only include a small fraction of the vast numbers that exist. To attempt to seriously collect all buttons of all categories - without any constraining discernment - would surely be an overwhelming undertaking. Most collectors therefore identify particular aspects of personal interest, and limit their button acquisitions accordingly. Many themes arise from this approach including those included below.

## Era

The most popular "period" buttons are the Victorian pieces. These evocatively record the many and varied uniformed organisations of this exciting and productive era of British history.

## Heraldic Achievements

Many organisations have used heraldic achievements within the design of their buttons, particularly municipal authorities and scholastic bodies. The buttons within this collecting theme provide scope for some interesting research.

## Geographically Related

This theme includes buttons relevant to counties, cities etc. As an example, see the interesting notes compiled by John Richman (page 87) to complement his Portsmouth collection.

## Backmark Varieties & Variations

Themes concerning identified manufacturers, tailors etc (see Chapter 5 page 72).

## Material Make-Up

Some collectors, in appreciation of high quality specialise in, for example, silver Sheffield plate buttons. Others find natural horn has special appeal and, of course, mounted pieces are favoured by many.

## Makers

Of the many button makers, Jennens & Co is a bygone firm whose high standard of workmanship particularly encourages collection. This firm produced consistently high quality pieces from 1800 until 1924 when it was merged with Gaunt & Son.

## Specialist Subjects

The most popular area of theme collecting is that of "Specialist Subject" study, such as banks, hospitals, golf clubs and so forth. However, there are nine subjects in particular that represent the most popular themes with plenty of button examples falling within each classification. These are the buttons of: Household Liveries, Public Road Transport, Railways, Police Forces, Fire Brigades, Yacht Clubs, Hunt Clubs, Scholastic Bodies, and Shipping Lines. In light of the very high interest in these subjects, by way of additional examples to those given in Chapter 1, a further selection is included on pages 83, 85 & 86. This material is preceded below by supporting notes in respect of the early "button years" within each of these subjects. (NB It will be seen that "Theme Subject" classifications do not necessarily "align" with the categories used in Chapter 1 of this book.

### I. Household Livery Buttons

These are reviewed in Chapter 3.

### II. Public Road Transport Buttons

The use of horse drawn buses and trains ceased at the beginning of the 20th century when the combustion engine and overhead electric lines took over (trolleybuses came into limited use in the 1930s). However, in the 1950s both trolleybuses and trams were withdrawn, leaving motorbuses only (apart from taxis) to serve as public road transport with services being run by both private and Corporation operators. Early issue buttons struck in either white metal or brass have been replaced by chromium plated ones. Many private companies used one-word abbreviations for the motif on their buttons (ie **C.1**, "General" standing for the London General Omnibus Company).

## III. Railway Buttons

Following the Railway Act of 1844, passed to regulate the activities of competing railway companies, growth of the industry was nevertheless such that by 1921 there were 120 companies operating in the national network. However, the Railway Act of that year sought to rationalise the situation by amalgamating these into just four organisations: The London Midland & Scottish, The London & North Eastern, The Southern, and The Great Western railways. These in turn were nationalised in 1948 to form British Railways, which has since been fragmented and privatised.

Many of the early buttons, which were struck in either brass or white metal, had motifs comprising only representative initials (eg **C.5**, **C.7**, and **C.9**).

C5

C7

C9

## IV. Police Force Buttons

Since the formation of the Metropolitan Police Force by an Act of Parliament in 1829, up to 1974 there have been 10 further Acts affecting England and Wales covering the police force establishment and various amalgamations and mergers. These measures condensed constabularies into 41 County and Area forces plus the Metropolitan and City of London forces. (In addition there are those police not controlled by the Home Office such as The Manchester Ship Canal Police).

A great variety of police buttons has been produced over the years, and in 1934 chromium plated ones were introduced; however, the more recent issues do not bear the distinctiveness of the early ones.

## V. Fire Brigade Buttons

Fire fighting services before 1939 consisted of Town, City and Volunteer brigades but, with the threat of war the Auxiliary Fire Service was instituted to supplement these services. In 1941 this arrangement was superseded by the establishment of the National Fire Service, which prevailed until 1948 when County Authorities were then made responsible for fire and rescue services. In 1974, as part of Local Government reorganisation, the Fire Services were subjected to reorganisation too. Many of the uniform buttons since 1948 are of designs identical to those of colleague Ambulance Brigades, and most bear the Coats of Arms of their administering Local Authority.

## VI. Yacht Club Buttons

Many yacht club buttons reflect prestigious associations, for most clubs were founded during Queen Victoria's reign when yacht owning was highly fashionable for the wealthy and those in the ranks of high society. Many of these clubs have the privilege of "Royal" in their titles because of the patronage they enjoyed, and perpetuate the Victorian royal crown version or Prince of Wales' Feathers within their buttons' designs. The buttons are mainly of gilt finish, but some are of blackened bronze, or made of black horn or composition, the metal pieces being generally notable for their high quality. Very widely featured are the traditional "rope" rims and anchor motifs.

## VII. Hunt Club Buttons

Hunt Clubs are numerically dominated by Foxhound hunts but also include Staghounds, Beagles, Bloodhounds, Basset hounds, Harriers, Drag hounds, and at one time Otter hounds. The earliest button examples date from the 18th century. Some clubs have two button types - one for field wear, the other for dress wear - while lady members usually have buttons of black horn. Hunt buttons are noted for their high quality, particularly the early issues.

Club buttons are not only "badges" of membership, but also denote proficiency; for they are normally only awarded to riders of a certain ability. Their designs mostly comprise the club's initials, although some include peers' coronets where the master is so elevated.

## VIII. Scholastic Buttons

Charity Schools in early Victorian times led the way in the adoption of uniforms, followed by the newly formed Public Schools. In the latter case, however, uniforms were intended as an expression of high social status. Grammar schools fell in line, with uniforms intended to distinguish their pupils from the non-uniform possessing Elementary and Secondary schools. Besides buttons for general wear blazers, special button versions have been produced for school Sports and Old Boy Societies, Cadets and even porters' uniforms. Blazers are not so fashionable as they once were, and tend not to be worn these days by University and College students; but they are still readily obtainable. Scholastic buttons mostly bear respective Coats of Arms (ie **C.29**, **C.30 and C.32**.

C29

C30

C32

## IX. Shipping Line Buttons

The transition from wind sail to steam power in the 1840s coincided with the new demand for mail carrying, which necessitated regular service routes. This, combined with an increase in requirements for passenger and goods conveyance to distant parts of the world, gave rise to an expansion in the number of shipping lines operating in late Victorian times.

Shipping Line buttons, with "roped" rims, anchor motifs and Company flags abound. They are mainly of gilt finish, but of silver finish in some cases for those employed as members of the purser's crew staff. Collectors of shipping line buttons often embrace worldwide issues, and associated marine pieces too.

## PUBLIC ROAD TRANSPORT

**C.1** London General Omnibus Company

**C.2** Thames Valley Traction Co Ltd

**C.3** Blackpool Corporation Tramways

**C.4** Derby Corporation Tramways

## RAILWAYS

**C.5** Southern Railway

**C.6** Pensnett Railway

**C.7** Great Western Railway

**C.8** Pullman Catering Staff

**C.9** Kent & East Sussex Railway

## POLICE

**C.10** West Mercia Constabulary

**C.11** City of London Police

**C.12** Devon Special Constabulary

**C.13** Manchester Ship Canal Police

**C.14** Liverpool Police

## FIRE BRIGADES

**C.15** Birmingham Fire Brigade

**C.16** Perth and Kinross Fire Brigade

**C.17** London Fire Brigade

**C.18** City of Winchester Fire Brigade

C1-C18
GENERAL
C1
THAMES
VALLEY
C2
BLACKPOOL CORPORATION
TRAMWAYS
C3
CORPORATION TRAMWAYS
C4
S.R
C5
C6
GWR
C7
C8
K&ESR
C9
WEST MERCIA
CONSTABULARY
C10
C11
C12
MANCHESTER SHIP CANAL POLICE
C13
C14
BRIGADE
C15
C16
C17
CITY OF WINCHESTER
C18
CM

## YACHT CLUB BUTTONS

**C.19** Norfolk and Suffolk Yacht Club

**C.20** Royal Southampton Yacht Club

**C.21** Royal Southern Yacht Club

**C.22** Royal Yacht Squadron

## HUNT CLUB BUTTONS

**C.23** Tedworth Hunt

**C.24** Vine Hunt

**C.25** Tiverton (Staghounds) Hunt

**C.26** Whadden Chase Hunt

**C.27** Sir Watkin Williams-Wynn's Hunt

## SCHOLASTIC BUTTONS

**C.28** George Heriot's School

**C.29** Oxford University

**C.30** St Dunstan's College

**C.31** Eton Archery

**C.32** Taunton School

## SHIPPING LINE BUTTONS

**C.33** Ellerman Bucknell Line

**C.34** The Aberdeen Line

**C.35** Port Line

**C.36** GPO Telegraph Dept. (undersea cable laying)

C19-C36
C23
C28
C19
C33
SS
C24
C29
C20
C34
SAINT · DUNSTANS · COLLEGE · CATFORD
1888
C25
C30
C21
C35
C26
C31
C22
C36
TAUNTON SCHOOL
C27
C32
CM

## Miscellaneous Black Composition Buttons

**C.37** Salvation Army member's button

**C.38** Royal Society for the Prevention of Cruelty to Animals inspector's button

**C.39** Automobile Association patrolman's button

**C.40** Flint and Denbigh Hunt Club lady's field coat button with white inlay

**C.41** General Nursing Council for England and Wales button

**C.42** The Boys' Brigade members' button

**C.43** British Red Cross Society members' top coat button (late pattern)

# Appendix

The following information, which has been compiled by John Richman on the geographical button collecting theme of Portsmouth, serves as an example of how research can enhance the "button interest factor". The reference numbers refer to the line drawings of actual specimen buttons.

**Collecting Themes - Portsmouth**

The sheltered waters of Portsmouth harbour have provided a safe haven for ships since before Roman times. The **Anglo-Saxon Chronicle** records the landing of Porta and his two sons at *Portes Mutha* in AD 501. The town's first recorded charter was in 1194, and dates back over 800 years. The star and crescent, which features on many Portsmouth buttons, is a prominent part of William de Longchamp's seal. He was Richard the Lionheart's Chancellor, and the motif represents a direct link with the Crusades.

Portsmouth became a Borough in 1835, taking on responsibility for law and order, fire fighting, health and general improvements in sanitation. City status was granted in 1926. St Thomas', which became the Cathedral, has only recently been enlarged.

**Police and Fire Services**

The Police Force, as in many towns, was responsible for fire fighting. Records show that the Fire Brigade was grossly inadequate for many years, relying heavily on Naval and Military garrisons for help (see Figs.2.-5.).

**Transport**

The first horse trains ran from the railway station to Clarence Pier in 1865. This was the first statutory tramway in this country. The system was taken over by the Corporation in 1901 (see Fig.6.) when the first electric tram ran. The last horse tram ran in 1904 and the last electric tram in 1936. Buses, first used in 1919, lasted until deregulation. Trolley buses were used from 1934 until 1963.

Fig.1.

Fig.2.

Fig.3.

Fig.4.

Fig.5.

Fig.6.

Fig.7.

Fig.8.

Fig.9.

Fig.10.

Fig.11.

Fig.12.

Fig.13.

Fig.14.

**Hospitals**

The mental hospital was opened in 1879. Its various titles over the years reflect changes in attitude towards mental health:-

1879 - Borough of Portsmouth Lunatic Asylum
1920 - Portsmouth Borough Mental Hospital (see Fig.7.)
1926 - Portsmouth City Mental Hospital
1937 - St James' Hospital for Nervous & Mental Diseases (see Fig.8.)
1960 - St James' Psychiatric Hospital

**Yachting & Leisure**

Lord Fitzclarence, son of the Duke of Clarence (later William IV), was instrumental in having an area of marsh and scrubland cleared when he was Governor of Portsmouth. A promenade and pier were built for the locals, the pier opening in 1861 (see Fig.9.). Further along the promenade the Royal Albert Yacht Club (see Fig.10.) opened in 1864. Other yacht clubs, mainly located near the harbour mouth, include the Portsmouth Sailing Club (1875), The Royal Portsmouth Corinthian Yacht Club (1880) see Fig.11., Portsmouth Yacht Club (1932) see Fig.12., Portsmouth & Southsea Motor Boat Club, and Locks Sailing Club.

**The Navy**

The Royal Navy has had a very strong presence in "Pompey" for many centuries but, apart from **HMS Excellent**, the Gunnery School on Whale Island, it is necessary to look at backmarks to get local connections. I have recorded these: J. Friedeberg, Portsea; H. Martin & Son Ltd., Portsmouth; Matthews & Company, Portsmouth; Moseley & Pounsford, Portsmouth. (See Figs.13. & 14.).

# Bibliography


**Baily's Hunting Directory**, J. Allen & Co, London.

Briggs, G. **Civic & Corporate Heraldry - A Dictionary of Impersonal Arms, Ramsbury 1971**.

**Burke's Peerage Baronetage & Knightage**.

*Button Lines,* the quarterly journal of the British Button Society, miscellaneous articles.

**Councils, Committees & Boards**, CBD Research Ltd.

**Directory Of British Associations**, CBD Research Ltd.

**Debrett's Peerage & Baronetage**

Fairburn, J. **Crests Of The Families Of Gt. Britain & Ireland**, New Orchard Editions, London.

Fox-Davies, Arthur Charles, **A Complete Guide To Heraldry**, Bracken Books, London.

Harrison & Sons Ltd, **Dress And Insignia Worn At His Majesty's Court**.

Macmillan Press, **The Royal Encyclopedia**

Meredith, Alan and Gillian + Michael J. Cuddeford, **Identifying Buttons**, Mount Publications, 1997.

Pine, L.G., **A Dictionary Of Mottoes** Routledge & Kegan Paul, London.

Ripley, H., **Police Buttons**, R. Hazell & Co, Henley-on-Thames.

Squire, Gwen, **Buttons A Guide For Collectors**, Frederick Muller Ltd, London 1972.

Squire, Gwen, **Livery Buttons The Pitt Collection** Leghorn Co., Pulborough 1976.